# Told Tales
## Nine Folktales from Around the World

Retold by
### Josepha Sherman

Illustrated by
Jo-Ellen Bosson

All Folktale Introductions and Activities by
Betsy Loredo and Wendy Wax

SILVER MOON PRESS
New York

First Silver Moon Press Edition 1995

For information contact:
Silver Moon Press
126 Fifth Avenue
Suite 803
New York, NY 10011
(800) 874-3320


Project Editor: Eliza Booth
Designer: John Kim


Library of Congress Cataloging-in-Publication Data

Sherman, Josepha.
Told tales : nine folktales from around the world / Josepha Sherman ;
illustrated by Jo–Ellen Bosson. – 1st Silver Moon Press ed.
p. cm. –(Family Ties)
Includes bibliographical references.
Contents: Creation tales: Coyote makes the world. Why the sky is
separate from the earth—Hero tales: The laidly worm. Stupid head. Li Chi
and the serpent—Moral tales: The fisherman and the slave. Necessity. The
story of Ifan—Silly tale: Hiding the bell.
ISBN 1-881889- 64-5 (hard) : $12.95
1. Tales–Cross–cultural studies 2. Heroes–Folklore. 3.
Creation–Folklore [1. Folklore 2. Heroes–Folklore. 3. Creation–Folklore] I.
Bosson, Jo–Ellen, 1941- ill. II Title. III Series: Family ties (New York, NY)
GR69.S52 1995
398.2–dc20         94-49621
CIP


10 9 8 7 6 5 4 3 2 1
Printed in the USA

*II*

# TABLE OF CONTENTS

*III*

# INTRODUCTION

When someone older than you tells you a story, listen. The story might be thousands of years old! Why have stories lasted so long? Storytellers keep them alive. A storyteller is anyone who enjoys listening to, remembering, and passing on good stories from one generation to the next. You probably have one or more storytellers in your family. In fact, you might even be one yourself!

Every time someone repeats a story, it changes slightly. This is because storytellers like to add details of their own. If your grandmother and father tell you the same tale about a princess, your grandmother might call her Elizabeth, while your father calls her Anabel. Though each version shares the same basic story and moral, or overall lesson, some of the small details are different.

Folktales have many versions. The one you hear depends on who the storyteller is and where the tale is from.

Stories don't just travel from generation to generation—they travel from country to country, too. A Chinese teacher in France might tell a Chinese folktale to her students. And a Mexican family living in Australia might tell Mexican tales to its friends and neighbors. Sometimes, the same tale will be found in many countries all over the world—then, the tale is called a "world folktale." People come to the United States from every country in the world. Just think of all the folktales they bring with them. This is how tales travel. In fact, people often say that folktales have wings and fly!

There are many types of stories. Some are filled with magic, while others are more realistic. The oldest stories explain how the world began. Others tell exciting adventures of heroes and villains. Some tales end with important morals, while others are silly and make you laugh.

So get ready to enjoy the special tales retold in this book by folklorist Josepha Sherman.

~~Stop~~

When you're finished reading, you might try telling them on your own. How will you begin? What new details will you add? Remember  Once you become the storyteller, the way you tell the tale is up to you.

2

# Two Creation Tales

# COYOTE MAKES THE WORLD
## NORTH AMERICA

INTRODUCTION

*In the Beginning*

D id you ever wonder when the earth began? How animals were made? Where people came from? If you asked your mother or father, what do you think they would say? Chances are, they'd have a "creation tale" to tell.

All creation stories are thousands of years old. Early storytellers told them to explain things they didn't understand. It was their way of making sense of such things as how the earth was formed and where its creatures came from. What stories have you heard? Do you believe them? If someone asked you how the world began, what would you say?

You can learn about families by the creation stories they tell. These stories are often based on a family's religious beliefs or on the beliefs of a certain culture. A Jewish family's creation stories are different from those told by a family that practices Hinduism. A family that tells the story of Adam and Eve will most likely belong to a Judeo/Christian–based religion. And a family who believes that "Coyote" created the world might have Native American ancestors.

Some Native American children love to hear stories about Coyote, a trickster who is always getting into trouble. To them, Coyote is as familiar as Mickey Mouse is to you.

In "Coyote Makes the World," Coyote's curious nature leads him to create land, animals, and people. Why does he do it? Because without people and animals, who would he play tricks on?

## COYOTE MAKES THE WORLD
### [A Tale of the Crow People of North America]

N ow, no one knows where Old Man Coyote came from. He was just there, he and the wide waters and a few small ducks and other birds. And Old Man Coyote was bored.

"There is no one here for me to talk to except these silly ducks, no one to play tricks upon, no one here to do anything. There is nothing to see but water and more water, and nothing ever changes." Coyote shook his head. "I like change. This sameness will never do. I must find a way to put more excitement into the world!"

"Younger brothers," he called to the ducks, who were paddling about on the surface of the water the way they always did, "do you see anything different anywhere?"

"We see nothing but water," they told him.

"What about under the water?" Old Man Coyote asked. "Have you seen anything down there?"

The ducks thought and thought. "We might have seen something down there," they said at last. "But we never really took a good look."

"Well then, go down and look!" Coyote exclaimed.

The youngest duck dove. Down and down he went, and he stayed underwater so long Coyote began to think that he had drowned. But at last the young duck came popping back up to the surface. "Look," he mumbled, holding something in his beak. "Look what I have found."

"This is a root," Coyote exclaimed. "Surely that means there is earth under the water."

"What is earth?" the ducks asked.

"Never mind. Dive again, young brother. If you come upon something soft, bring it up to me."

So the young duck dove and brought up a beakful of mud. "Is this what you want?" he asked.

"This is exactly what I want!" Coyote cried. "This is mud, and this mud shall become our home."

He blew upon the little lump of mud, and it began to

grow larger and larger, spreading out over the water. The ducks all quacked in wonder. "Wait," Coyote told them. "There is more to come."

He planted the root the young duck had brought him into the soft mud. And grass began to grow from that root and plants and even trees. Coyote played with his new creation, pushing down the mud here to make valleys and piling it up there to make mountains. He made holes in it for fresh springs of water, and he cut paths for rivers to flow free.

At last Coyote sat back to admire his work. "This is wonderful!" the ducks quacked. "You are so clever, elder brother!"

"Not so clever," Coyote muttered. "There is still no one to talk to or play tricks upon. Ha! I know what I shall do! I shall give us some companions!"

So Coyote took up a handful of mud and made some animal–figures out of it, male animals and female animals; those that eat grass and those that eat meat; those that crawl on the ground and those that fly through the sky. Last of all, Coyote made people–figures out of the mud, though no one knows how he did it. The people–figures came alive, just as the animals and birds had done, and walked about, marveling at their new world.

"Now I've done it," Coyote said happily to himself. "Now there will be laughing and fighting and all sorts of things. Now there will be lots of change. Now I will never, ever again be bored!"

# WHY THE SKY IS SEPARATE FROM THE EARTH
## BOTSWANA

### INTRODUCTION
#### *Mothers and other Strong Women*

This next story is another type of creation story. When the story was first told, people didn't have the scientific knowledge that we have today—they didn't know that the sky is made of invisible gases. But that didn't stop them from making up their own stories about how the sky was created and how it related to the earth.

In stories like this one, it's not a special animal or a single creator who is responsible for making great changes in the world. Instead, the creators are people— in this case, they're women. Telling stories like these made people feel more powerful.

Women are the heroes in many stories, because they will do just about anything to protect or help their families. Women have always been important, powerful members of some African communities, which is how they came to be in tales from Africa. Some African tribes tell a story of a mother who tricked an animal into eating her—just so that she could travel into its stomach to rescue her children. She allowed the beast to swallow her whole!

In "Why the Sky Is Separate from the Earth," a woman gets tired of sitting around, waiting for something to happen. Instead, she decides to make a change herself.

## WHY THE SKY IS SEPARATE FROM THE EARTH
### [A Tale of the Nyimaing People of Africa]

In the long–ago days, the world was finally finished. Animals ran on its surface or burrowed into the soil, and fish swam in the seas. People lived on the surface of the world too.

Only one thing was still strange: the sky hadn't quite finished separating from the earth. No, no, it pressed down on everything like a too–low ceiling. This was no problem for the animals, who ran about on four feet and weren't very tall, but it made life very difficult for human beings, who stood up on two feet. Every time they tried to straighten up, they banged their heads on the sky!

*10*

Oh, but it was even worse than that. The sky would suddenly sag down lower in some places than in others, and there was no way to tell where or when this would happen.

In one place where a tribe of people had settled, the sky kept dipping lower and lower, until no one could stand upright. They had to walk about all bent over.

The women of this tribe used to make porridge out of millet seed, which they would stir in big pots with long stirring sticks. Unfortunately, the sky sagged so low one day that the women could barely cook their porridge. Those long stirring sticks kept getting knocked down by the low ceiling of sky. In fact, so close to the pots did the women have to hold their stirring sticks, that they kept burning their hands!

"Will no one help us?" they cried. "Will no one chase the sky away?"

The men shrugged helplessly. What could they do? Who could move the sky?

But just then, one woman burned her hand for the third time and cried out in anger. "I have had enough of this nonsense!" she shouted. "All I'm trying to do is cook dinner for my family but this stupid sky won't let me!"

Raising her stirring stick like a spear, she stabbed up at the sky with all her strength. Again and again, that angry woman stabbed at the sky and...she broke it! She broke the sky into a hundred small clouds that whirled away up into the heavens. As they flew, they faded and left the

*11*

people with a fine, high, endless ceiling of the clearest blue.

All the people scrambled to their feet with cries of wonder.

"Look! Look! We can stand without bumping our heads! Why even the very tallest among us can stretch their arms up as high as they can reach without touching the sky!"

"So they can," the woman said, calmly stirring her porridge.

"What are you doing?" the others cried. "Come celebrate. You are a hero!"

"No, I'm not," she said. "I'm a woman with a very hungry family." But she stopped stirring and smiled as she said it.

# Three Hero Tales

# THE LAIDLY WORM
## ENGLAND

### INTRODUCTION
*Good or Evil?*

Some of the most exciting stories are tales about good versus evil. These stories are often about a young boy or girl—often a prince or princess—who is being chased by an evil villain. The villain might be a witch, monster, troll, wolf, dragon, queen, or evil stepmother. Often, the villain knows magic. In "Snow White and the Seven Dwarfs," Snow White is the young girl and the jealous queen is the villain. What other stories do you know that have good and evil characters? Do they always end in the same way?

We can sometimes tell where a story comes from by the story's villain. Tales about Baba Yaga, a fearful witch

*15*

who flies through the air in a mortar or bowl, are from Russia. The evil stepmother is a villain popular in fairy tales and folktales from many countries. Usually, the stepmother is jealous of a stepchild, so she casts a spell that's almost impossible to break. In one fairy tale, an evil stepmother changes her stepsons into swans. In order to break the spell, their sister must weave thorns into seven shirts and may not speak for seven years in order to free them.

In "The Laidly Worm," a tale from England, an evil stepmother casts a horrible spell on her stepdaughter. When her stepson finds out, he uses his good magic against her evil magic. Can you guess which magic wins?

## The Laidly Worm
### [A Tale from England]

Once upon a time, there lived a king who had two children, a son known as Childe Wynd, and a daughter named Margaret. Childe Wynd grew up to be a fine young man and went off to seek his fortune, sure that his sister would be safe with his parents.

But alas, soon after Childe Wynd left, his mother died, and his father, in his grief, married too quickly. The woman he wed was lovely to see, but her heart was cold and jealous. When Margaret welcomed her to the castle, the new queen ignored the maiden's goodwill and saw only that Margaret was pretty. And that prettiness angered the queen. She did not want anyone to be half as fair as she.

Sadly for Margaret, her stepmother knew dark sorcery. That night, when everyone else slept, the queen worked her spell:

*I wish you to be a laidly worm*
*And free you never shall be*
*Till Childe Wynd, the king's own son,*
*Shall give you kisses three.*

And that, the queen told herself with a wicked smile, would never, ever happen. For who would dare kiss a laidly worm, an ugly dragon?

So it was that Margaret went to bed a human girl and woke up a hideous monster. Amid the screams of her servants, who were sure that the dragon had eaten the princess, she crept and crawled slowly out of the palace to hide herself upon a barren hilltop.

Meanwhile, word reached Childe Wynd that a laidly worm was laying siege to the land. And even though no one said that the worm had harmed a soul, the prince dared not wait. He hurried home as quickly as his ship would sail. But Childe Wynd had learned a tiny bit of magic—good magic—on his travels, so he made sure that the hull of his ship was of rowan wood, the wood no sorcery can touch.

Sure enough, when the evil queen saw in her enchanted glass that Childe Wynd was sailing home, she

summoned several nasty imps and told them, "Do what you will with that ship. Childe Wynd must not reach home!"

Off the imps fled. But the ship's hull was of rowan wood, they could do no harm, and at last they flew back to the queen and told her, "We cannot hurt him or his ship because of that rowan wood."

The queen cried out in fury and banished the imps. "If I cannot use the imps to stop him, I shall use his own sister against him!"

So she cast a spell that forced the laidly worm down to the shore. Three times Childe Wynd tried to land, three times the queen cast his ship back. At last, he ordered that the ship set out for sea again, and the queen, watching from her enchanted glass, laughed to see him surrender.

But Childe Wynd hadn't surrendered. Instead, he sailed his ship into a secret cove and rushed ashore, ready to do battle with the laidly worm. But she made not the slightest attempt to fight him. When he approached, his sword in hand, the laidly worm lay down before him. To Childe Wynd's amazement, she murmured:

> *Sheathe your sword, unbend your bow*
> *And give me kisses three.*
> *For though I am a laidly worm,*
> *No harm I'll do to thee.*

Could that possibly be his sister's voice? Or was this

the dragon's trick, so it might lure him close enough to eat him? Childe Wynd hesitated, but the laidly worm murmured:

> *Sheathe your sword, unbend your bow*
> *And give me kisses three.*
> *If I'm not freed ere set of sun,*
> *A worm I'll always be.*

"It is your voice, Margaret!" Childe Wynd cried. And before any of his men could stop him, he kissed the hideous monster once, twice, thrice. In a moment, he held not a laidly worm but his own dear sister in his arms.

Quickly, Margaret told her brother what had happened, and Childe Wynd hurried to his father's castle. The wicked queen tried her best to cast a spell on him, but Childe Wynd held a rowan branch, and the sorcery sprang back from him and struck the queen instead. Before the astonished eyes of all the court, she turned from a woman into an ugly little toad and hopped away. So much for her.

Childe Wynd and his sister, Margaret, lived long and happy lives.

# STUPID HEAD

## INDIA

⌒⌒

## INTRODUCTION
*Think Fast!*

H ave you ever heard a story in which a mighty creature—perhaps a lion—is outsmarted by a tiny creature—perhaps a mouse? You might answer "The Three Little Pigs," in which the third pig outsmarts the wolf by building a wolf–proof, brick house. Or you might answer "The Brave Little Tailor," in which a small tailor uses his wits to protect himself from a ferocious giant.

Tales like these are told all over the world. The characters often change from country to country, but each story has one thing in common—a hero who is able to overcome a much stronger person or creature by using his or her wits and thinking fast.

Often, it's the heroes who get themselves into trouble to begin with. They can't help it—they're just very curious. Luckily, the more curious people are, the smarter they will be in the end—one hopes, smart enough to save themselves in the face of danger. People who live in Chile tell stories about a hero known as Pedro Urdimales. In England, one heroine is a quick-thinking girl named Molly Whuppie. Who are the heroes in stories that you know?

Like heroes, mighty creatures also change from country to country. In Persian tales, the creature is often a ghoul that possesses amazing magical powers. In Norse tales, it's a fierce troll. What kind of mighty creatures are in the stories you know?

The hero in "Stupid Head," a tale from India, is Prince Rasalu. His curiosity leads him up a tall and mighty tree to meet up with Old Stupid Head, a high and mighty, but not too smart, goblint. How will the prince outsmart him? Read on and see.

## STUPID HEAD
### *[A Tale from India]*

Once, long ago, young prince Rasalu went for a walk in the forest by himself. He had become bored with life at court. For some time, the young man wandered here and there like any ordinary fellow, enjoying the sounds of birds and monkeys and the sight of many towering trees.

*But how far could I have walked?* he wondered suddenly. *I don't see anything I know.*

The day had grown so warm and the prince was so tired from all his walking that he sat down there and then, at the foot of one very tall tree, a tree so great that its leaves spread out over his head like a big green cloud.

Prince Rasalu rested for a time, listening to the birds all around him. Then, all at once, he straightened up.

"Those aren't birds' songs," he said aloud. "Those are people's voices. And they're coming from somewhere high in this tree! Now who, I wonder, can be living up there?"

He couldn't see anything through all those leaves. And so Prince Rasalu began to climb the tree to find out. It was a big tree, a mighty tree, a true tower among trees, and he climbed for long and longer still.

At last the prince broke through the cloud of leaves and found himself in a village! The villagers were rebuilding one of their houses, which were made from branches, and they called to the prince to stop and help them.

"I'm sorry," he told them. "I hear more voices higher in the tree, and I want to find out who is up there. Do you know?"

The villagers refused to answer, so Prince Rasalu began to climb once more, higher and higher. At last he found himself at the very top of the tree—and there

*23*

stood a gleaming palace.

*Who could possibly live up here?* the prince wondered. *The doors stand open. What if I look around?*

So Prince Rasalu entered warily, looking about for servants or guards. What he found instead were goblins, ugly creatures with long fangs. But all of them were sound asleep.

*There must be more than this,* the prince told himself, and tiptoed on.

In the uppermost room of the palace, he found a thick stone column. Bound to the column by a golden chain was a young woman. Prince Rasalu gasped. Surely she was the most beautiful woman he had ever seen in his life. He fell in love with her on the spot.

"Oh, at last!" the young woman cried. "I've hoped someone human would find his way up here. Hurry, set me free. I beg you!"

Prince Rasalu hastily looked for something to break the golden chain. In a corner stood a rusty ax, and he snatched it up and set about cutting through the chain.

"Who are you?" he asked in wonder. "Who bound you here?"

The young woman gave a mighty sigh. "I am Princess Balna. And the one who bound me here is Old Stupid Head, that's who! He's a goblin who wants me to be his wife. He's away from the palace today. Oh, hurry, free me!"

"There!" With one last cut of the ax, Prince Rasalu severed the chain. He took Princess Balna by the hand

*24*

and they ran from the palace and scrambled down and down the mighty tree.

"Stop!" the villagers called to them. "Where are you going in such a hurry?"

But the prince and princess didn't waste time in answering. They scrambled all the way down to the ground and hurried off through the forest.

Meanwhile, Stupid Head came flying back to the palace on his bat wings. What was this? All his guards were asleep and the princess was gone! With a roar of rage, the goblin went racing down the tree.

"Have you seen my princess?" he shouted at the villagers.

They pointed. "She went down the tree just a short time ago."

Off Stupid Head went, leaping and flapping his way down to the ground, roaring with rage as he went. So much noise did he make, that the prince and princess heard him and hid in the bushes.

"You say that he really is very stupid?" Prince Rasalu whispered.

"Very," Princess Balna said.

The prince grinned. "So be it," he said, and came out of hiding. As Stupid Head came rushing up, Prince Rasalu pretended to weep and wail.

"Ohhh!" he sobbed. "Alas, alas, alas!"

"Have you seen my princess pass this way?" Stupid Head asked.

"Alas, alas, oh, ohhh, alas!"

"I said *have you seen the princess?*" the goblin roared.

"I have s–seen no one," the prince sobbed. "M–my e–eyes are too–too full of–of tears!"

"I don't care about your tears!"

"Y–you should. Terrible news, oh terrible! Poor Stupid Head is sick. He's so sick, he's likely to–to die!"

"No!" Stupid Head gasped. "That's terrible news indeed! But, can it be true?"

Off he flapped, back to his palace, where he seized his goblin guards and shook them till their fangs rattled. "Am I sick?" he asked. "Am I sick enough to die?"

"No!" they cried. "You are not sick at all."

"Why, that lying human! I will kill him," screamed Stupid Head. And off he flapped again.

The prince and princess heard him coming and hid in the bushes. "It's working," Prince Rasalu whispered. "Wait here."

He took off his elegant silk cap and tousled his hair, then turned his fine silk jacket inside out. Stupid Head didn't recognize him.

"Have you seen my princess?" the goblin asked angrily. "And a weeping liar as well?"

"No, no, I have seen no one," Prince Rasalu said shortly. "I have no time to waste on such things. I am a royal messenger sent by the king, and I must hurry to Stupid Head's palace to tell his goblins the sad news."

"What sad news?" Stupid Head asked.

"Why, have you not heard? Poor Stupid Head is no longer ill—he is dead!"

"Dead?" Stupid Head asked. "Oh, no! Can this be true?"

Off he flapped towards his palace. Grabbing the first goblins he could find, he shook them and shouted, "Am I dead? Tell me, *am I dead*?"

"No!" they cried. "You are very much alive!"

Stupid Head roared with rage. "They tricked me! I-I-I'll kill them! I'll kill them both!"

Off he flapped—but by now, the prince and princess had almost reached Prince Rasalu's palace. Stupid Head flapped as fast as he could. The prince and princess ran as fast as they could. Now they were almost inside! Stupid Head grabbed at them, but Prince Rasalu's guards slammed the palace doors shut just in time.

Stupid Head crashed right into those doors. All he caught was a sore nose.

"That hurt!" he grumbled. "Humph. I didn't want that silly princess anyhow."

Still grumbling and rubbing his nose, Stupid Head flapped away, and Prince Rasalu and Princess Balna never saw him again.

And they, of course, lived happily ever after.

# LI CHI AND THE SERPENT
## CHINA

## INTRODUCTION
### *Clever Gretchen*

Princes and boys aren't the only ones who can beat a fearsome foe. Many times, the hero is a girl. Some stories with girls as the hero are called "Clever Gretchen" stories. The first Clever Gretchen stories were told in Europe and were about a heroine with that name. Has anyone in your family ever told you a Clever Gretchen story?

At the beginning of most Clever Gretchen stories, the heroine's family tries to keep her safe at home, but she doesn't listen. Instead, she bravely sets off to face the dangers on her own. She'd rather face death than pass up an opportunity to protect her family or neighbors from the enemy. How can a young girl defeat a giant, life—threatening foe? By using her wits and tricking her evil opponent.

In other tales, girls use bravery and resourcefulness, not trickery, to save their families from evil villains. "Li Chi and the Serpent" is a tale from China in which a maiden named Li Chi realizes that something must be done to save the women in her village—and she's just the one to do it!

## LI CHI AND THE SERPENT
### [A Tale from China]

O nce, in ancient days, in the Kingdom of Yueh, a terrible serpent came to live in the Yung Mountains. There it coiled around the rocks and sent dreadful dream messages to everyone—*I will destroy the land and all the people if I am not given maidens to eat.*

Oh, the wailing and moaning that followed the hearing of this threat. What could the people possibly do?

"We can't let our maidens be eaten!" they cried.

So the people sent for brave heroes to kill the serpent for them. The heroes swaggered boldly up to the mountain peak. But when they saw the serpent, with its terrible fangs and claws, every one of those heroes ran away.

"Enough delay!" the serpent roared at the people. "I

*30*

will destroy you all if I am not given maidens to eat, and quickly!"

"What can we do now?" the people wailed. "We have no heroes left! We will surely have to give the serpent the maidens it wishes."

And so, a hunt for maidens began. Word of this dreadful search reached the family of a poor farmer, Li Tan. Li Tan had once been a soldier, but that had been long ago. Now he was a father with six daughters, and his old sword hung on the wall, slowly rusting.

When Li Tan and his daughters heard about the serpent, they began to weep at the thought that one of them might well be chosen to be eaten.

Only the youngest of the six daughters, Li Chi, did not waste time weeping. "Why should I cry about something that might never happen?" she told her father. "And I refuse to let myself be frightened of a creature that I have never seen!"

Instead, Li Chi began to wonder just how such a monster might be stopped. And an idea came to her.

"Let me be chosen," she told her father.

"No!" he cried in horror.

"Yes," she insisted. "Only be sure the officials who come for me give you a nice ransom in exchange for me. That way, no matter what happens, my sisters will have some money on which to live. Oh, Father, don't worry. I have no intention of letting myself be eaten. And I have no intention of letting any other girls be

eaten either!"

The officials came for her very soon. "I will come with you," Li Chi said humbly. "But first, let me take a memory of home with me."

So she took her father's rusty sword, the farm's snake—hunting dog, and a sack of sweet rice with her. She let the officials lead her up to the mountain peak. There, Li Chi seated herself comfortably and began rolling the sweet rice into tasty treats. These she placed at the entrance of the serpent's cave. Then she hid in the shadows to wait, holding the snake—hunting dog so that he would not whine or bark.

The serpent smelled the sweet rice and came out of the cave. Oh, but he was terrible to see with teeth sharp as spears and eyes bright and fierce as flames. Hiding in the shadows, Li Chi bit her lip to keep from crying out in fear.

The serpent paused, looking down at the sweet rice. *What is this? These strange objects smell interesting, indeed!* After a wary look around, he lowered his head and began to eat.

"Now!" Li Chi whispered to the dog, and let him loose. The serpent smelled just like a snake to the dog, and he bit the monster with all his might. The serpent roared in surprise and whirled toward the dog—and as he did, he left his long neck exposed. Li Chi raised her father's sword and struck down with all her strength, cutting that serpent's head right off.

"You will never eat another maiden," Li Chi said, and went home.

Word of Li Chi's feat reached the King of Yueh. He went to visit her father's farm. He liked what he saw of Li Chi so much—and she liked what she saw of him, too—that he made her his queen. She and all her family lived happily at court from then on.

And no other monsters ever troubled the Kingdom of Yueh again.

# Three Moral Tales

# THE FISHERMAN AND
# THE SLAVE
## SPAIN

### INTRODUCTION
*Unexpected Rewards*

I f you believe that stories were created to teach children lessons, you're right—and wrong! Many of the stories we tell today were originally created for adults, not children.

In India, there is a collection of lesson–teaching stories called the Panchtantra. These tales were first created to teach princes the lessons they would need to rule over vast empires. Children still hear these stories today and can learn from their morals just like the princes did.

If your parents have learned important lessons from old stories, they'll want to share those stories with you so you can learn what they did. If they want to teach you to be generous, they might tell a tale about Robin Hood, who stole from the rich and gave to the poor. It can be much more interesting and fun to learn a lesson through a story filled with magic and danger than it is to be told what to do.

Many stories teach that when you do a good deed, you'll be rewarded in unexpected ways. In a tale from Tibet and many other countries, animals help a hunter, who has freed them, to perform dangerous tasks. In another world tale, a ghost helps a boy who has protected his dead body from grave robbers. And in one of Aesop's literary fables, a lion remembers a mouse who did him a favor. What can be learned from these stories?

Other stories teach what happens to those who aren't grateful when a debt is repaid. The good deed is often reversed and the ungrateful person is horribly punished. This might be a pretty harsh lesson, but it's important.

Reading or listening to a story like "The Fisherman and the Slave," a tale from Spain, can be a lot more interesting than having someone tell you to "do unto others as you would have others do unto you." You'll probably agree.

THE FISHERMAN AND THE SLAVE
*[A Tale from Spain]*

Once, in the long–ago days, Spain was not yet one country. Instead, the lands were divided into kingdoms, some ruled by Spanish kings, others by Moorish emirs who had come from North Africa. The Spanish and Moors were enemies who often fought and made slaves of each other.

Now, in those days, there lived a peaceful Spanish fisherman named Ramon. Ramon was a wise fisherman who knew where to find a good harvest of fish and how best to sell what he caught. And though he wasn't rich, he wasn't poor, either. And because he was a good–hearted fellow, on every feast day, Ramon would look for a poor man to treat to a fine meal.

"Tomorrow is Christmas," he told himself. "I must look for the poorest man I can find, for surely he'll be the greatest in need of a good meal."

So out Ramon went, hunting for his guest. But instead of a Spanish beggar, he found a Moorish slave, half starved and miserable.

"The Moors are the enemies of my people," Ramon mused. "I should turn my back on this fellow."

But Ramon couldn't turn away. Try though he would, he could not see this unhappy man as an enemy. No, no, this was just another human being who had fallen on hard times.

"Who are you?" Ramon asked.

The slave looked at him in surprise. "I am called Hamid."

"Well, Hamid, every feast day I find a poor man to feed. Would you like to come home with me this day?"

Ramon took the slave home with him and fed him well. After the meal, the two men sat and spoke together for a little while. They talked of small things, happy

things. They even laughed together. And to Ramon's surprise, he found himself starting to like Hamid. There was only one thing the Moor would not mention, and that was who he had been before he had been taken as a slave.

In the morning, the slave went back to his master. But soon after, Ramon heard that Hamid's family had paid a ransom for him.

"What a fine thing!" Ramon exclaimed. "Now he's free and back in his country."

He went back to his own life as a fisherman and forgot about Hamid.

A year passed. One day, Ramon was fishing far out at sea when he saw a ship on the horizon. "A pirate ship!" he gasped. "A Moorish pirate ship!"

What could he do? Ramon spread the sail on his boat and started for home as quickly as the wind could carry him. But his boat was small and its sail couldn't catch much wind. Soon the pirate ship loomed over his little boat, and Ramon knew he was lost.

Sure enough, the pirates took Ramon to North Africa, to a Moorish city, where he was sold as a slave. Ramon sat in chains in the slave market, waiting unhappily for someone to buy him. He never even looked up at the wealthy man who came to look at him. What difference did it make who bought him? He would still be a slave. And he had no rich family to ransom him!

Suddenly Ramon realized that someone was staring at him. He looked up and saw a Moor clad in silken robes that glittered with gems. Surely this was some great nobleman.

"Are you not a fisherman?" the Moor asked.

Ramon shrugged. "I was."

"And is not your name Ramon?"

"Yes, but—"

"And did you not one day take a poor Moorish slave into your home and feed him? Come, my friend, don't you know me?"

Ramon blinked. "Hamid!" he cried.

"You were kind to me, Ramon, when no other man even said a gentle word to me. You were kind to me without a thought of reward or a worry that our people are enemies. And now I shall repay that kindness."

With a commanding wave of his hand, he brought the slave dealer running to remove Ramon's chains. "You are free," Hamid told the fisherman. "I shall put you aboard my own swift ship and see that you are safely returned home. Oh, and take this, my friend." He pushed a purse, heavy with gold, into Ramon's hands. "Share this with other poor folks in memory of our friendship."

And so Ramon did. And never did he or Hamid forget each other.

*41*

# NECESSITY
## ROMANIA

## INTRODUCTION
### A True Test

What can you do this year that you weren't allowed to do last year? Can you stay up later than you used to? Can you cross a big street by yourself? As you get older, your parents will allow you to do more and more things on your own. They know that it's all a part of growing up.

Many stories are about growing up and taking on more responsibility. Usually these stories are about a boy who is about to become a man or a girl about to become a woman. Before the child is allowed to move on, he must pass a sort of test, given by someone older. This often happens in real life, too—with parents.

Parents might "test" their daughter to see if she is ready to stay home alone. At first they'll only leave for a little while. If everything goes okay, their daughter "passes" the test, and next time she can stay alone longer. Other parents might "test" their son to make sure he's ready to walk to school by himself. If everything goes okay the first few times, he'll be rewarded with the privilege of walking to school alone every day.

What if you fail your parents' test? There is no way to fail. Your parents will love you even if they feel you are not ready. They'll also give you plenty of other chances to prove yourself. But the reward of being ready is that you'll be able to do something new all the time.

In "Necessity," a tale from Romania, a boy is being tested by his father and he doesn't even know it. He has to rely on his wits to help him out of trouble. Would you be ready for a test like that? What new things do you think you're ready to do?

## NECESSITY

*[A Tale from Romania]*

Once there was a farmer who was blessed with all a farmer could wish for: fine, fertile lands, happy, healthy animals, a comfortable home, and a handsome son, Petr. Petr was a good–natured young man and as loving a son as ever a father could wish for.

But because everything went so well on the farm, he knew nothing at all of hardship and want.

His father worried about that. "Petr has never experienced even the slightest bit of ill–luck. I don't even know if he could be clever enough to fend for himself if something went wrong! No, no, this will never do. I must find a way to test my boy and see if he can, indeed, overcome some hardship," he said to himself.

From that day on, the farmer gave Petr all the difficult jobs to do, all the tasks that might possibly go wrong. But nothing went wrong!

"This will never do," the farmer mused. "I must find some way to test Petr."

He thought about it and thought about it. Then, late one night, the farmer woke with a laugh. "Ha! I have it! I know exactly how I'll test my Petr."

So the next morning he called his son to him and said, "Petr, I wish you to go on an errand for me."

"Of course, Father. What is it you need?" the son replied.

"I wish you to go into the forest and look for necessity."

Petr frowned. He assumed his father meant for him to go and find a person. But Necessity! That was an odd name for anyone to bear. "And where will I find Mr. Necessity?"

"Don't worry, my boy. If you don't find necessity,

necessity will surely find you and teach you a wise lesson. But I don't want you to come home before that happens. Do you understand? You are not to come home until you have found necessity or necessity has found you."

Now Petr was more confused than before. Was the mysterious Necessity a friend of his father's?

Whoever he was, he must be a clever fellow indeed, if he could find someone in that vast forest! "Very well, Father," Petr said reluctantly. "Let me take a horse and—"

"No, no," his father interrupted. "We need all the horses today."

"Then I shall take a sturdy oxcart and—"

"No, no, we shall need all the sturdy oxcarts as well. Here is what you may take."

He led the boy to the most rickety, most worn-out oxcart on the whole farm. "This?" Petr asked. "B–but it will surely fall apart the moment I enter the forest."

"Don't worry," his father said with a smile. "If it does fall apart, necessity will help you fix it."

And so a truly puzzled Petr drove his two oxen off into the forest, the rickety old cart rocking and creaking beneath him. He drove far and long into the forest, till the tall trees nearly shut out the light with their leaves and he could barely see his way. And all the time he rode, Petr called out: "Mr. Necessity? Mr. Necessity? Can you hear me? Please, Mr. Necessity, I'm looking for you!"

*45*

But no one answered. The day wore on, and the night came near, and Petr looked around uneasily. The forest was a very wild place, full of wolves and bears that might want to eat a team of oxen. Or even a boy!

"Mr. Necessity! Please!"

Just then, the oxcart struck a rock and tilted sideways so suddenly that Petr was thrown to the ground. As he picked himself up, the boy groaned.

"Look at this cart. One of the axles has snapped right in half, and there's the wheel, rolled off by itself." Petr glanced about with a shiver. He was alone, all alone in the middle of the wild forest. *And there isn't a glimpse of Mr. Necessity. Now what am I going to do?* the boy wondered to himself.

He sat down on a rock, with his head in his hands, until the oxen, who had been peacefully nibbling on leaves, straightened up with a snort. Petr straightened, too. What was that? Had he heard wolves howling?

"I can't stay here and wait for Mr. Necessity. Father was wrong; he's nowhere around. I can't walk all the way back home, not with the night almost here. So I'll just have to fix the cart myself. But how?"

Petr walked around the cart. The wheels looked all right, but the axle was definitely broken.

"There are many stray branches lying around. I wonder..." Petr thought aloud. He used his belt knife to whittle off a good, straight branch that looked to be the right size.

"Now, how do I hoist the cart up so that I can get the broken axle off and the new one on?" He paused and then said, "I think I know."

Petr took another branch, a strong, springy one. He balanced it on a rock, slipped one end of the branch under the cart, and stood on the other end. Sure enough, the branch acted as a lever, and the cart bed came up off the ground. Petr braced the branch with another rock, so the cart wouldn't fall on him, and set about pulling off the broken axle and slipping in the new one. He fixed both wheels firmly onto the new axle, then let the cart settle back to the ground.

"It worked! The new axle is holding!"

Petr jumped back onto the cart and picked up the reins. "Come, my oxen. Let's go home!"

Meanwhile, Petr's father was pacing back and forth, forth and back. Had he done the right thing, sending his boy off into the forest? Here it was, nearly night, and there wasn't a sign of the boy.

Ah, but here he comes! Here comes Petr now! The farmer looked at the newly repaired cart and beamed. "My boy, my clever, clever boy, you did find necessity!"

Petr frowned. "I did no such thing. I saw no one in the forest at all, most certainly not any Mr. Necessity. And he didn't teach me a thing! All I learned was that if something needs to be done, you cannot just wait around for someone else to do it. You have to help yourself."

*47*

The farmer laughed. "My dear boy, I never meant for you to find a *man* named Necessity! I just wanted to be sure that you could solve problems by yourself. And now I can be proud because necessity has taught you a fine lesson after all.

# THE STORY OF IFAN
## WALES

## INTRODUCTION
*Good Advice*

Who is the oldest person you know? Is it your grandmother or your grandfather? Is it a great-grandparent? After living such a long life, this person probably has many stories to tell and advice to give. If you're smart, you'll listen to the stories and follow the advice. In most cultures, respect for elders is very important because age brings experience, and experience brings wisdom. Have you ever taken advice from an older person? Was it helpful?

In many stories, as well as in real life, old people who have a business often hire apprentices. An apprentice is someone who works for an older person—sometimes for money, and sometimes to learn a skill. A tailor teaches his apprentice how to shorten clothing, sew on buttons, and wait on customers. A doctor teaches his apprentice to use medicine, learn diseases, and help patients. And a magician teaches his apprentice how to use magic. Getting hands–on experience on a daily basis is often much more valuable than reading about a business in a book—especially when working under a greatly respected teacher.

In "The Story of Ifan," a tale from Wales, a poor young man named Ifan is hired as a farmer's apprentice. Instead of paying his apprentice in wages, the farmer pays him with two pieces of strange advice. What will happen if Ifan follows the advice? Is he brave enough to try it out and see?

## THE STORY OF IFAN
### *[A Tale from Wales]*

One day, in a long–ago time in Wales, work grew scarce and a young man named Ifan was forced to leave his wife at home and go far afield looking for someone to hire him. He came to a house of a wise old farmer, who asked him, "What can you do?"

Ifan shrugged. "Any work that needs to be done."

So they shook hands on the agreement of three pounds for a year's work, and two years of work all told. Things went well, for Ifan was an honest laborer and the farmer was a good man, and, at last, the two years were up and done.

"Which would you rather have?" asked the wise old man. "Your wages, and that being the end of it, or two pieces of advice, one for each year?"

Ifan hesitated. He wanted those wages, indeed he did! And he wanted to be off and home to his wife. But in two years, he had come to respect the wisdom of the farmer. Surely his words would be worth hearing. "Tell me the advice," Ifan decided.

The farmer smiled as though Ifan had passed an important test. "One rule," he said, "is this: Never leave the old road for the new one."

Ifan frowned, wondering if maybe he'd made a mistake. "And the second?"

"The second: Always remember that honesty is the best policy."

Ifan frowned even more deeply. Surely he should have asked for his wages instead. Too late, too late. "Well, thank you, I'll be leaving now."

"Wait. Take this loaf home to your wife, and when you are most joyous together, break open the loaf and remember me," the wise old farmer said.

So Ifan set out on the road for home. Along the way, he came across three merchants, who greeted him cheerfully. "And where are you going?" they asked.

"Home to my wife," Ifan said.

"This road is the long way about. Come with us—we

know a shorter way."

But when they came to the head of the new road, Ifan remembered the wise old farmer's warning.

"I'll stick to the old road," he told the merchants.

And it was well he did. Robbers were waiting on the new road. They stripped the merchants of all they had, and no doubt they would have killed poor Ifan outright for having no wealth upon him.

Meanwhile, Ifan reached home and was greeted joyfully by his wife. "I've been so lonely for you," she cried.

"And I for you. But what is this?"

A heavy leather purse lay in the dust of the road near his house. Ifan picked it up and frowned. "Isn't this the crest of our good duke?"

"It is," said his wife. "The purse must have fallen from his saddle when he and his men rode by here yesterday."

Ifan peeked inside and whistled. "It is full of gold coins," he said, turning to his wife. "My love, if we keep this, we would want for nothing."

"But we would be thieves," his wife murmured.

Ifan remembered the wise old farmer's advice and sighed. "Honesty is the best policy," he muttered. "You're right. We'll go together to the duke's castle and return it to him."

So off they went to the castle. But they could not get in to see the duke. "Oh, no," the snooty servant told them. "You must leave the purse with me, and I will see that the duke receives it." Ifan and his wife went home sadly.

Now, as it happened, the duke went hunting the very next day. He stopped near Ifan's house to drink from the well, and Ifan's wife asked, "Did your lordship regain his purse?"

The duke frowned. "What's this? I was given no purse."

The duke brought Ifan and his wife to the castle. They pointed out the servant who had taken the purse, and sure enough, there it was among his belongings.

"You are a thief!" the duke thundered, and had the man cast out of his service. And because Ifan and his wife were so honest, he hired them on the spot.

No longer poor, happy in his home in the castle, Ifan remembered the loaf the wise old farmer had given him.

"He told me to break it open only when we are most joyous together," Ifan told his wife. "Surely there can be no better time."

So he broke open the loaf and burst into laughter. For inside the loaf were six pounds, his wages for the two years of service.

# ONE SILLY TALE

# HIDING THE BELL
## GERMANY

## INTRODUCTION
*Silly Town*

I magine living in a place where every person acts silly all the time. Would you feel out of place? Or would you join in and act silly, too?

Many cultures tell stories about a certain town in which foolish people live. Sometimes the towns really exist, and sometimes they don't. If they do exist, the people who really live there don't act as silly as the people in the stories. The people in stories don't try to act silly at all. In fact, most of the time they think they're being clever—which only makes the story funnier.

Depending on where they are from, people from different cultures often find different things funny. But sometimes a story is so funny it doesn't matter where it's told. One such world tale is about a married couple who have a contest—the first one to speak loses. Neither person wants to lose, so they watch their house get robbed in silence. Another story is Hans Christian Andersen's classic literary tale "The Emperor's New Clothes." You've probably heard it. When the silly emperor, who thinks he's fully dressed, parades through town wearing no clothes, do you laugh?

Jewish families tell stories about silly people who live in the town of Chelm. Mexican families tell stories about silly people from the town of Lagos de Moreno. And German families tell stories about people in the village of Schwarzenborn.

"Hiding the Bell," a tale from Germany, takes place in Schwarzenborn. In this story, the foolish people are all so sure they're being clever that they don't even realize their silly error—they mistake it for a victory!

## HIDING THE BELL
### [A Tale from Germany]

The people of the little town of Schwarzenborn were not fools. No, just as it was with the people of Chelm, it was simply that sometimes they saw things a little differently from the rest of the world.

Now, it happened that in Germany one time there was a terrible shortage of metal. No tools could be made without metal, and the soldiers had no guns to carry. And so a proclamation went out all over the country. People must turn in any metal they really didn't need to the government, so it could be melted down and made into more useful things.

News of this proclamation reached Schwarzenborn. Oh, what excitement! No one in the town could think of anything else but the metal they did not really need.

*What can we give to the government?* they wondered.

"Aha!" cried Hans, the grocer. "I know what we can do. We can turn in our plows."

"But how will we plow our fields?" Otto, the farmer, asked timidly.

That was a problem.

"Maybe we can turn in our axes." Herman, the candlemaker, suggested.

"Then how will we chop wood for our fireplaces?" Hans asked.

That was a problem too. The people of Schwarzenborn sat and thought. What could they give the government? What metal did they have that they didn't really need?

One by one, everyone looked up at the church steeple. In that steeple hung a bell, a wonderful bell, a marvelous bell—but a bell most certainly made of metal.

"Oh, no," said Hans.

"Oh, no," said Otto.

"We can't give up our bell," said Herman. "Not our wonderful bell with its nice, rich sound."

"Not our wonderful bell that cost so many coins," added Hans.

"But the government will send men," Otto moaned. "Men to collect metal from our town. They will most surely see the bell, and they won't care what a nice, rich sound it has or how many coins it cost. No, they will take our bell from us—they'll melt it down!"

"We can't let that happen," the folks of Schwarzenborn decided. "We must keep the government from taking our lovely bell away."

"But how are we going to stop them?" Hans asked.

"We must hide the bell!" everyone cried.

"But where can we hide it?" Otto wondered. "What if we just throw a blanket over it?"

That sounded good to everyone. But then Hans asked, "Won't it look strange to the government? A blanket in a steeple, I mean?"

"Oh, dear," said Herman. "That won't do. We must take the bell down from the steeple and hide it somewhere else."

But where could they hide it? The people of Schwarzenborn tried to hide the bell under some straw. But the bell was so big, there wasn't enough straw to cover it. They tried to dig a hole big enough to bury it. But no one could decide what to do with all the earth they had dug out—the only place they could find to put it was back in the hole they had dug!

"I know what to do!" Hans said suddenly. "There's only one thing we can do. We must hide the bell in the one place no one would ever think of looking. We must hide it in the lake!"

Everyone cheered. What a wonderful idea! They pushed and pulled the heavy bell into a boat, and Hans and Otto rowed it out into the middle of the lake. With much struggling, they managed to push the bell out of the boat and into the water. Oh! What a wondrous splash it made! In a moment, the bell had sunk from sight.

"We've done it!" Hans and Otto cried in joy. "We've hidden the bell!"

But all at once, Otto stopped smiling. "We forgot one thing, Hans. Once it's safe to get the bell again, how are we going to remember where we hid it?"

That was a problem. Hans and Otto were silent for a long time trying to solve it. How could they remember where in the lake they had hidden the bell?

"I have it!" Hans cried. "And it's so simple. Otto, to remember where we hid the bell, all we have to do is mark the spot by putting a notch in the side of the boat!"

So they did, and all the people of Schwarzenborn rejoiced that their bell was safely hidden.

# TALE TELLERS

Folktales are mostly told by professional folklorists. However, tales are also passed along by many other people...

Tales are told in families.

Tales are told among friends.

Tales are told in religious ceremonies.

Tales are told without words–through mime.

Tales are told through song.

*63*

# ꓮCTIVITIES

## TRACKING DOWN TALES

If your family members do not tell stories, it doesn't mean they do not have them. Sometimes parents don't think that the stories they heard when they were children will be interesting to their own kids. How can you discover these important parts of your family's culture and history? Just ask! Here are some ideas to keep in mind when you're tracking down your family's tales:

• A family story does not have to feature dragons, fairies, or evil stepmothers. It can be tales of bravery by an uncle or aunt during wartime, or tales of grandparents' survival against impossible odds. Your family's favorite tale might be the story of a wedding where everything went wrong or an adoption where everything went right. A story can feature a kind stepmother who does something funny to win over her new family. When you ask your family to tell their tales, remind them that these stories count, too. Perhaps in a thousand years, your mother's daring deeds will be told in a book of classic folktales.

• Sometimes the people who pass down the family stories live too far away to tell them to you in person. Don't let that stop you. Ask your family, especially grandparents and older relatives, to tell their stories to a tape recorder or video camera. If your family does not feel comfortable performing, suggest they read you their favorite tales from books. This usually loosens up people, even those with the worst stage fright. The best part of putting your relatives' tales on tape is that you can then share them with other family members and friends as well.

• Staple pages of paper together to make a small book. Or buy a book with blank pages from a store. Then write your family stories down and illustrate them. You can also write your family stories into a computer and use drawing programs to illustrate the stories. One great way of decorating your told tales is with collages.

• Here are some techniques for good collages: Scrounge through your house to find objects that reflect your family members, and mount the objects on paper, cardboard, or even wood. Other collage materials are cutouts from magazines, postcards, labels, stamps, sand, shells, small toys, fabric scraps, wood scraps, buttons, string or yarn, dried foods like

*65*

macaroni or beans, toilet paper tubes, doilies, aluminum foil, waxed paper, plastic wrap, and colored paper scraps. Your collage can be very specific, like one that shows a scene from a story. Or it can illustrate the feelings you had when you first heard the tale.

## MASK MAKER

Although the stories they tell may be different, there is something many cultures share—the use of storytelling masks. A terrifying dragon face, with glistening green scales, hisses a warning. The round, moon–like face of a fairy rises from the waters of a deep lake. The bright eyes of a brown bear shine as he bows his head before a hunter. Masks of these characters help storytellers get every inch of the thrills, chills, and magic from their stories.

The following directions will help you make your own storytelling mask. Decorate it to match the character of one of the stories in this book or one of your own family's tales that you have tracked down.

### MAKING THE MASK
*You will need*:
- A medium–weight paper plate (non plastic–coated)
- A tongue depressor or popsicle stick
- Tape
- Scissors
- A dull–tipped pencil
- Decorations for the mask: markers, paints, crayons...

*66*

*Directions:*

- Using your scissors, cut two slits in the middle of the plate. Cut from the edge toward the center. The slits should be about two inches long. Later, you will overlap these edges so that your mask bends out a bit in the center. That way, your mask will cover your face better and have a three–dimensional quality.

- Use the dull pencil to poke two holes in the mask where you want your eyes to be. Poke the pencil in and jiggle it around to make holes big enough for you to peer through.

- Decorate the front of your mask, using your markers, crayons, or paints. If you like, you can use glue to add feathers, glitter, sequins, cloth, or strips of colored paper.

- Attach the tongue depressor to the back of the mask. Use tape to secure the depressor. You will use the stick to hold the mask in front of your face.

- On the sides of the mask, overlap the edges of the slit an inch or so until the mask bends outward. Tape or staple the overlapped edges in place.

- Create masks for each character in your story or just one or two for special effects.

*Now tell your story!*

# FOLKLORIST'S NOTES

### COYOTE MAKES THE WORLD

Coyote is a very important character in the myths and folklore of Native American tribes of the western half of the United States. He is the type of character known as a "trickster," a being who plays tricks on everyone and who loves to see things change. Coyote is neither good nor bad; he is sometimes a creator, the way he is in this story, but he can also be a destroyer or just someone who enjoys a good practical joke.

### WHY THE SKY IS SEPARATE FROM THE EARTH

This story shows that sometimes great deeds can be done, not by a great hero, but by an ordinary person who is fed up with things the way they are. There are not too many stories about the sky hanging low down over the earth and needing to be separated. The ancient Egyptians told how the sky and the earth loved each other so fiercely that the gods were forced to tear them apart so that life could exist on earth.

## THE LAIDLY WORM

This story is known in two forms—both as a folktale and as a ballad dating back to the Middle Ages. Although most stories about dragons, particularly those from western Europe, feature dragons as villains, there are a few, such as this one, that tell about good people who have been transformed into dragons, usually by an evil wizard. There are a good many stories about evil stepmothers! The word "childe" does not mean that Wynd was not an adult; it is an ancient word meaning "young man" and was often used in old ballads as part of a young man's proper name. "Laidly" is an ancient word, too, meaning "loathsome" or "hideous." And "worm" is an old term meaning "dragon." Folklore about the rowan tree, which is also known as mountain ash and has bright red berries in autumn, says that it has great power against sorcery.

## STUPID HEAD

This story comes from the Kashmir region in India, and was written down in the nineteenth century but is probably much older. The Indian tree that Prince Rasalu climbed is much like the English Jack's magic beanstalk, with a village and a mysterious palace hiding in its branches. There are many stories from around the world about magic realms that are found at the tops of trees or the bottoms of wells. In many stories about goblins or devils, the evil creatures are described as being very stupid, so stupid that they can be convinced of almost anything—even that they are dead.

## LI CHI AND THE SERPENT

This Chinese tale is one of the earliest that was written down. It dates from the Chin Dynasty, which lasted from the third to the fourth centuries A.D. Unlike the dragons in European folklore, Chinese dragons are usually good creatures and sometimes very powerful beings who control the rain and the water. And so, instead of a dragon, the monster in this story is a giant serpent. He sounds like a European dragon, though, with his hunger for the flesh of maidens. Yueh is not a kingdom nowadays, but a province within China.

## THE FISHERMAN AND THE SLAVE

This tale dates from the Middle Ages when Spain was made up of many small kingdoms, sometime between the tenth and fourteenth centuries. In those days, part of Spain was ruled by Spanish Christians, and a good deal of the land was ruled by Muslim emirs who had come to the country from Morocco and other parts of North Africa. Even after Spain became one country, and the Muslims were cast out, Moorish pirate ships continued to sail the Mediterranean until the sixteenth century.

*70*

## NECESSITY

We have a saying in America that is similar to the theme of this Romanian story: "Necessity is the mother of invention." It means that we are often most creative when forced to be so by a need. There are several folktales throughout the world in which a character mistakes a notion such as necessity—or an emotion such as fear—for a living person and goes looking for—or running from—that person.

## THE STORY OF IFAN

This tale may date from the Middle Ages, although it was written down in the nineteenth century. The idea of "honesty is the best policy" is known throughout the world. Many folktales feature a nobleman's servant who turns out to be a thief or a liar while the hero, often a common fellow, proves to be worthy of merit. Ifan (or Ivan or Iwan) is the Welsh version of the name John.

## HIDING THE BELL

Schwarzenborn has a whole series of silly tales that were told about the people who lived there. But this particular story has been told by people all around the world, from China to North America. Good stories get around!

# BIBLIOGRAPHY

Afanas'ev, Aleksandr, *Russian Fairy Tales*. New York: Pantheon Books, 1945.

Ausubel, Nathan, *A Treasury of Jewish Folklore*. New York: Crown Publishers, 1948.

Bierhorst, John, *The Red Swan: Myths and Tales of the American Indians*. New York: Farrar, Straus & Giroux, 1976.

Briggs, Katherine M., *A Sampler of British Folk-Tales*. London: Routledge & Kegan Paul, 1977.

Dorson, Richard M., *Folktales Told around the World*. Chicago: University of Chicago Press, 1975.

Erdoes, Richard, and Alfonso Ortiz, *American Indian Myths and Legends*. New York: Pantheon Books, 1984.

Feldman, Susan, *African Myths and Tales*. New York: Dell Publishing Company, 1963.

Hayes, Barbara, and Robert Ingpen, *Folk Tales and Fables of the World*. New York: Portland House, 1987.

Jacobs, Joseph, *Celtic Fairy Tales*. New York: Dover Publications, 1968.

————, *English Fairy Tales*. New York: Dover Publications, 1967.

Jagendorf, M.A., *The Merry Men of Gotham*. Eau Claire, Wisconsin: E.M. Hale & Company, 1950.

Manning-Sanders, Ruth, *A Book of Princes and Princesses*. New York: Dutton and Company, 1969.

Parades, Americo, *Folktales of Mexico*. Chicago: University of Chicago Press, 1970.

Radin, Paul, *African Folktales*. New York: Schocken Books, 1983.

Ramanujan, A.K., *Folktales from India*. New York: Pantheon Books, 1991.

Ranke, Kurt, *Folktales of Germany*. Chicago: University of Chicago Press, 1966.

Roberts, Moss, *Chinese Fairy Tales & Fantasies*. New York: Pantheon Books, 1979.

Sproul, Barbara, *Primal Myths: Creating the World*. New York: Harper & Row, 1979.

Van Over, Raymond, *Sun Songs: Creation Myths from around the World*. New York: New American Library, 1980.